W9-CTP-453

Cornerstones of Freedom

The Battle of Antietam

Zachary Kent

CHILDRENS PRESS®
CHICAGO

Copyright 1992 by Childrens Press®, Inc.
All rights reserved. Published simultaneously in Canada.
Printed in the United States of America.
1 2 3 4 5 6 7 8 9 10 R 01 00 99 98 97 96 95 94 93 92

Library of Congress Cataloging-in-Publication Data

The Battle of Antietam / by Zachary Kent.
    p. cm. — (Cornerstones of freedom)
    Summary: Describes the events surrounding the bloody
confrontation between Union and Confederate troops in
the Maryland countryside on September 17, 1862.
    ISBN 0-516-06657-9
    1. Antietam, Battle of, Md., 1862—Juvenile literature.
[1. Antietam, Battle of, Md., 1862. 2. United States—
History—Civil War, 1861-1865—Campaigns.]
I. Title. II. Series.
E474.65.K46 1992
973.7'336—dc20
                                                    92-12097
                                                        CIP
                                                         AC

Musket barrels glinted in the sunlight as thousands of blue-clad Union soldiers tramped the country roads of Maryland. Horses snorted as squads of cavalry trotted ahead. Long lines of supply wagons churned up clouds of dust. The Union Army of the Potomac was on the march in September 1862. A few days earlier, the Confederate Army of Northern Virginia, commanded by General Robert E. Lee, had crossed the Potomac River into Maryland. Now Union Major General George B. McClellan was moving his troops north from Washington, D.C., in blind pursuit of the Confederates.

Confederate troops crossing the Potomac in September 1862

Confederate soldiers setting up camp after a long day of marching

On the morning of September 13, the Twenty-seventh Indiana Regiment halted for a rest outside the town of Frederick. The weary Union soldiers gladly stacked their muskets in a nearby field. Some men gathered firewood for boiling coffee. Others dropped onto the grass and closed their eyes. Relaxing together, Corporal Barton W. Mitchell and Sergeant John M. Bloss gazed idly over the littered ground. Just a few days before, Confederate troops had used the same field as a camp.

Corporal Mitchell noticed a rolled piece of paper lying within easy reach. When he picked it up, he made a happy discovery. The paper was wrapped around three cigars. As Sergeant Bloss unrolled the paper, he noticed that there was writing on it. Suddenly, his eyes widened. The paper was headed "Special Orders No. 191, Headquarters, Army of Northern Virginia, September 9, 1862." The two soldiers had found a lost copy of Robert E. Lee's Confederate military plans.

Mitchell and Bloss jumped to their feet and took the important document to their colonel. Within minutes, the paper reached General McClellan's headquarters. The Union commander

Robert E. Lee (left) and George B. McClellan (right)

scanned it and threw up his arms with joy. "Now I know what to do!" he exclaimed. "Here is a paper with which, if I cannot whip Bobbie Lee, I will be willing to go home. . . . It gives the movement of every division of Lee's army." McClellan used his lucky information and hurried his soldiers onward. The chase would end beside a peaceful Maryland creek called Antietam. On September 17, 1862, the Union and Confederate armies would clash there in the American Civil War's bloodiest single day of fighting.

A modern-day photograph of Antietam Creek

Slaves gathering cotton on a southern plantation in the early 1800s

Since 1861, the United States had been gripped by civil war. A long, raging argument over slavery and states' rights had torn the country in two. In the North, where factories thrived, thousands of European immigrants were willing to work for low wages. Most northerners had no use for slavery, and many considered it cruel and immoral. In the South, however, cotton was the major crop. It was grown on large plantations worked by African slaves. The southerners depended on slavery for the success of their farming economy.

The Civil War began with the Confederate attack on Fort Sumter.

Abraham Lincoln

The election of Abraham Lincoln as United States president in 1860 brought the problem to its final crisis. Angry southerners feared that Lincoln, a northerner from Illinois, would abolish slavery. They insisted that the federal government had no right to force laws upon the individual states. Rather than submit, eleven southern states decided to leave the Union. Together they formed the Confederate States of America, with Jefferson Davis as their president.

In April 1861, Confederate cannons bombarded Fort Sumter in the harbor of Charleston, South Carolina, forcing the withdrawal of the Union garrison. As war began,

President Lincoln called for volunteers to put down the rebellion. He vowed to hold the United States together at all costs. Soon the land shook with the crack of musket fire and the crash of thundering cannons. Some of the hardest fighting occurred on Virginia battlefields. In battle after battle, charging Confederates turned back Union advances on the Confederate capital of Richmond. On August 29, 1862, the two sides clashed again at the Second Battle of Bull Run. After two days of bloody combat, the beaten Union army streamed back to Washington, D.C.

After his victory at Bull Run, fifty-five-year-old General Robert E. Lee boldly started moving his

Jefferson Davis

Union troops in retreat after the Second Battle of Bull Run

Confederate Army of Northern Virginia northward. On September 4, the first detachment of his forty thousand soldiers waded across the Potomac River and invaded Maryland. Lee guessed that the rich farmlands of that border state would help keep his hungry soldiers fed. The need for foreign supplies and support also influenced Lee's decision. If the Confederates could win a major battle on northern soil, perhaps Great Britain and other European nations would recognize southern independence.

News of Lee's Maryland invasion caused great alarm in the North. President Lincoln depended on thirty-seven-year-old Major General George B. McClellan to find and destroy the Confederate troops. Cautiously, McClellan started moving the eighty-four-thousand-man Union army of the Potomac north from Washington, D.C., into Maryland. Then, on September 13, the copy of Lee's special orders fell into the Union general's hands. The wires hummed as McClellan telegraphed excitedly to Lincoln, "I have all the plans of the rebels, and will catch them in their own trap."

Now McClellan knew that Lee had split the Confederate army into at least four segments. Three groups, totaling about twenty-two thousand men, were heading west to surround and capture the large Union garrison at Harpers Ferry, Virginia. With the rest of his troops—about

*After invading Maryland, General Lee decided to make his stand in
the quiet countryside outside the town of Sharpsburg.*

eighteen thousand men—Lee was striking north
toward Pennsylvania. From McClellan's
headquarters, messengers galloped away to
deliver new Union orders. If the Federals moved
fast, they could crush the Confederate army one
section after another.

On September 15, Robert E. Lee and his
Confederates reached the country town of
Sharpsburg, Maryland. Sharpsburg lay on a fork
of land between the wide Potomac River and
Antietam Creek. Rolling hills, farmlands, woods,
and thickets covered the few miles of this point

A typical Confederate soldier of 1862

of land. Crossing the Antietam, General Lee gazed ahead and announced, "We will make our stand on those hills." Soon, word arrived that Confederate troops had captured the Harpers Ferry garrison, twelve miles away. Lee sent orders for the Confederate army to come together. While General McClellan wasted two full days bringing his huge Union army into position, most of the Confederate troops arrived. North of Sharpsburg, gray-uniformed Confederates took up positions along the dusty road of the Hagerstown Turnpike. Just east of the little town, southern troops crouched along the grassy ridges. Farther south, the thin Confederate defense line followed the lazy twists of gurgling Antietam Creek. Outnumbered two to one, the southerners braced themselves for the coming fight.

The men of the Second Rhode Island Infantry, shown here drilling in 1861, were among the Union troops who arrived to fight at Antietam.

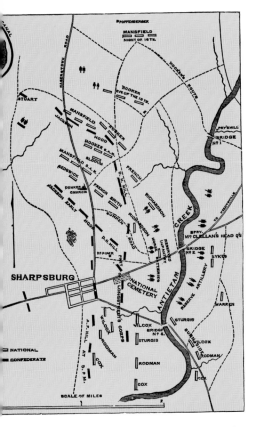

Left: A plan of the Battle of Antietam
Above: General Hooker's troops cross Antietam
Creek on the eve of the battle.

The rumble of cannonfire awakened the two armies before dawn on September 17, 1862. Following General McClellan's battle plan, Major General Joseph Hooker eagerly marched his Union First Corps forward through two woods, soon called the "North Woods" and the "East Woods," near the Hagerstown Turnpike. Ahead stood the tall stalks of farmer D. R. Miller's thirty-acre cornfield. Looking farther to the south across the turnpike, the northern troops spied a small, whitewashed building. On Sundays, members of the German Baptist Brethen—also known as the Dunkers—worshipped in this simple church.

Joseph Hooker

With a shout, Hooker's bluecoats charged toward the distant Dunker church and the "West Woods" that surrounded it. Suddenly, volleys of musket fire exploded from Miller's cornfield. Regiments of Confederates knelt among the ripe green stalks, loading and firing. Many Union soldiers screamed and clutched at wounds, while others cursed loudly and pushed onward through the swirling gunsmoke. The enemies smashed together fiercely. New Yorkers, Pennsylvanians, and Massachusetts men fired at Georgians, North Carolinians, and Louisianans. "Men were knocked out of the ranks by dozens," Major Rufus Dawes of Wisconsin later recalled.

An engraving depicting hand-to-hand combat at Antietam

Union troops charging toward the woods past the Dunker church

At last, the southerners retreated across the Hagerstown Turnpike and into the West Woods. With wild cheers, the Union troops climbed the roadside fences and charged toward the trees and the Dunker church. All at once, the red fire of a new Confederate musket volley staggered the northern troops. Confederate Major General Thomas "Stonewall" Jackson was sending in the last of his reserves; twenty-three hundred men commanded by Brigadier General John Bell Hood. Hood's furious counterattack stunned the northerners. They scrambled back across Miller's cornfield. During the next half hour, the savage fighting seesawed back and forth among the trampled cornstalks. By 7:30 A.M., the graycoats

John Bell Hood

These Union artillerymen, posing here between the East and West woods after the battle, saw savage fighting near the Dunker church.

Joseph Mansfield

still clung to their position. The bleeding survivors of Hooker's First Corps fell back and would fight no more that day.

The Union Twelfth Corps, however, hurried forward through the broken Union ranks and into the East Woods. Many of these raw recruits had never heard the noise of battle before. Galloping to the front, Twelfth Corps commander Major General Joseph Mansfield feared that a Maine regiment was shooting at some of Hooker's men by mistake. "Those are Rebels, General!" one soldier called out. Mansfield rode ahead to get a better look. "Yes, yes, you're right!" he exclaimed, as gray-clad soldiers suddenly opened fire. One bullet hit Mansfield's horse. The white-haired general tried to escape on foot. As he climbed over the fence, a musketball smacked into his stomach. Four Union soldiers quickly carried their dying leader from the field.

Brigadier General A. S. Williams took command of the Union Twelfth Corps. Past bloody bodies and splintered trees, the bluecoats charged out of the East Woods and onto the Miller farm. Some men later guessed that the battle surged back and forth across "The Cornfield" at least fifteen times that day. Bullets hissed through the air, and artillery shells ripped the ground. The thinned ranks of Hood's Confederate division fell back across the road to Woods.

the barns and sheds of the Samuel

A. S. Williams

Wounded Confederates lie in crude tents set up at the edge of a field during the battle.

Parks & History Association   Jul 10/95
  Antietam National Battlefield
  Bookshop
  P.O. Box 158 Highway 65 North

Qtv   Price   ISBN/PKU   Total
----
  1   3.95 0516-46657-7 KENT
        BATTLE OF ANTIETAM   3.95

                 Subtotal   3.95
Maryland Tax: 5%   0.20

                 Total   4.15
  1 Units Sold
Sales No.53461 Dr.ID 1   CASH $5.00
KS   @17:13   Cha.: $0.85

Confederate gun crews fire upon General Sumner's advancing troops.

Mumma farm, which lay south of the East Woods. Charging through the smoke, Brigadier General George Greene's brigades of the Union Twelfth Corps slammed into the Confederates who were defending that part of the battle line. Blistering musket volleys staggered the Union ranks. Fiercely, the Union troops rolled forward, firing volleys of their own. A few bluecoats reached the Dunker church before General Greene called a halt. By 9:00 A.M., badly broken up, the Union Twelfth Corps had done its best.

General Lee realized that the entire left side of the Confederate defense line might collapse at any moment. Quickly, he issued daring orders,

calling for a rapid shift of soldiers. From the
right side of the Confederate line, more than
three divisions of troops hastened north through
the streets of Sharpsburg. At the same time,
General McClellan sent more Union troops into
the fight. Crusty old Major General Edwin
Sumner rode at the head of the Union Second
Corps. Impatient for battle, Sumner charged his
lead division across the Hagerstown Turnpike
and into the West Woods. Suddenly, sheets of
flame burst from among the trees. Lee's
reinforcements had reached the West Woods in
time. The southerners screamed their high-
pitched "Rebel yell" and fired on the Union

Edwin Sumner

19

troops from three directions. "My God! We must get out of this!" shouted General Sumner in shock.

In a fearful frenzy, the Union soldiers struggled to escape. Cannon shells burst overhead and musketballs tore without mercy into the ranks of blue. "In less time than it takes to tell it," reported Massachusetts Lieutenant Colonel Francis W. Palfrey, "the ground was strewn with the bodies of the dead and wounded." Within twenty minutes, the northerners lost more than two thousand men. The dazed survivors of Sumner's attack staggered from the battlefield.

The noise of battle quieted along the left side of the Confederate defense line. After four hours of furious combat, the fighting shifted. Instead of following Sumner into battle, Brigadier General William French's division of the Union Second Corps lost its way. As French's troops crossed the Mumma farm and the nearby farm of William Roulette, sharpshooters fired on them from the center of the Confederate line. French advanced his soldiers in that direction.

To the south, an old country road zigzagged between the fields and pastures. Local people called it the Sunken Road because years of use by heavy wagons had worn it down. In this natural trench, the men of Major General D. H. Hill's Confederate division crouched and waited. They cheered as General Lee rode along the line. Lee told them that they must hold or the battle

General Lee was cheered when he rode along the Confederate line (left) to tell his men that they must hold the Sunken Road (above) or the battle was lost.

was lost. "These men," answered Colonel John B. Gordon of the Sixth Alabama Regiment, "are going to stay here, General, till the sun goes down or victory is won!"

Shouted orders and rattling drumbeats brought the Union troops into battle formation. With flags unfurled, French's men, four lines deep, marched over a ridge and across open fields toward the Sunken Road. Nearer and nearer they came to the waiting southerners. "Now the front rank was within a few rods of where I stood," Colonel Gordon described afterward. "With all my lung power I shouted, 'Fire!' Our rifles flamed and roared in the

John B. Gordon

Federals' faces like a blinding blaze of lightning."

Rows of northerners dropped, but French hurried more men forward. As musketballs whistled all around, the brave but outnumbered Confederates weakened. Four bullets wounded fiery Colonel Gordon in the arms and legs. Still, he continued to yell commands until a fifth bullet struck him in the face and knocked him to the ground, unconscious. At last, the Confederate line broke. The Union troops poured into the captured Sunken Road and saw Confederate dead piled two and three deep all around them. Never again did soldiers refer to the awful place as the Sunken Road. Instead, they called it "Bloody Lane."

After the battle, the Sunken Road was remembered as Bloody Lane.

The Union troops charged after the retreating southerners. "Men, put on the war paint!" screamed Colonel Edward Cross to his New Hampshire regiment. The men smeared their faces with black gunpowder. "Give 'em the war whoop!" Cross yelled next. A mighty roar filled the air as the soldiers rushed forward through a cornfield. West of the Hagerstown Turnpike, Confederate General James Longstreet tried frantically to pull a new line of defense together. Sweating Confederate cannoneers loaded and fired twenty artillery pieces as fast as they could. Shrieking shells tore into the charging bluecoats. One shell fragment struck Union General Israel Richardson in the side, inflicting a wound that would later prove fatal. By 1:30 P.M., the Union advance in the center of the Confederate line had lost its momentum. Though General McClellan had more than twenty thousand fresh Union troops nearby, he cautiously held them in reserve. Instead, the battle again shifted farther to the south.

Late in the morning, Union Major General Ambrose Burnside had at last received orders for his Ninth Corps. His eleven thousand men were to attack westward across Antietam Creek and break the Confederate right flank. Several Union brigades searched up and down the stream for easy crossings. The shallow Antietam could have been waded almost anywhere if the northerners

Ambrose Burnside

23

Robert Toombs

had bothered to try. Instead, General Burnside marched most of his men toward a sturdy, twelve-foot-wide stone bridge. Beyond the bridge rose a high bluff covered with rocks and trees. Only 550 sharp-eyed Georgians commanded by Brigadier General Robert Toombs defended this part of the Confederate line.

The Eleventh Connecticut Regiment began the Union attack, charging to the water's edge and ducking behind a low stone wall. Confederate cannon shells screeched overhead. Toombs's men peppered the Connecticut troops with deadly musket fire. Within fifteen minutes, one-third of the regiment lay killed or wounded. Next, the Second Maryland and Sixth New Hampshire regiments rushed toward the bridge with fixed bayonets. Confederate cannon blasts and Georgian bullets mowed down rows of the bluecoats. The dazed survivors soon stumbled away to safety.

Union Colonel Edward Ferrero commanded both the Fifty-first Pennsylvania and Fifty-first New York regiments. Shortly after noon, the dapper officer announced to his men, "It is General Burnside's special request that the two Fifty-firsts take that bridge. Will you do it?" With wild cheers, the Union soldiers ran toward the Antietam. Musketballs spit back and forth across the water as Union Captain William Allebaugh led the way onto the narrow bridge. The

Edward Ferrero

The outnumbered Confederates fought off several fierce charges before Burnside's men managed to cross the stone bridge over Antietam Creek.

northerners crossed the span in a mighty rush and swarmed up the bluffs. General Toombs and his steadfast soldiers finally retreated.

Most of the Union Ninth Corps filed across the bridge that would be known forever after as "Burnside Bridge." Downstream, other Union troops splashed across the creek at a shallow crossing called Snavely's Ford. Burnside's troops re-formed their battle lines, refilled their cartridge boxes, and prepared to charge.

Fewer than twenty-five hundred Confederates held the open ground in front of Sharpsburg. General Lee had stripped this part of his line in order to defend the West Woods and the Sunken Road. If Union troops captured the town and cut off the route of escape to the Potomac River, the Confederate army would be destroyed. Lee knew that Major General Ambrose P. Hill's Light Division, the last of the Confederate army to leave Harpers Ferry, was hurrying to Sharpsburg. Lee could only pray that these troops would arrive in time.

At 3:00 P.M., Burnside's Union Ninth Corps, still more than eight thousand men strong, moved forward across the open fields. "The earth seemed to tremble beneath their tread," one anxious southern officer later recalled. The

Burnside's men move across the open field toward Sharpsburg.

Sharpsburg residents take refuge in a cellar during the battle.

massive Union line crossed pastures and
scrambled past haystacks. "Now they rise up and
make a charge for our fence," Virginia private
John Dooley later recounted. "Hastily emptying
our muskets into their lines, we fled back
through the cornfield." Bullets skimmed the
grass as the northerners surged forward.

By 3:30 P.M., all seemed hopeless for the
Confederates. Retreating graycoats jammed the
streets of Sharpsburg. Suddenly, General Lee
noticed soldiers approaching on the road from
the south.

"Whose troops are those?" he asked an aide
who was looking through a telescope.

"They are flying the Virginia and Confederate
flags, sir."

This church on Main Street in Sharpsburg was damaged by artillery fire during the battle.

Ambrose P. Hill

It was General A. P. Hill's troops, arriving from Harpers Ferry, Lee realized with a sigh of relief. Dressed in the bright red shirt he always wore in battle, General Ambrose P. Hill ordered his three thousand troops to strike the unprotected left flank of the Union line. One startled Connecticut regiment lost 185 men within a few minutes. Many of the charging Confederates were wearing blue uniforms captured at Harpers Ferry. When Union soldiers of the Fourth Rhode Island Regiment saw bluecoats marching toward them, they held their fire. With rapid volleys, the disguised Confederates sent the Rhode Islanders reeling in panic. By sunset, Hill's Confederate counterattack had swept Burnside's Ninth Corps back to the bluffs along Antietam Creek.

After twelve long hours of fighting, the Battle of Antietam ended. It had been the bloodiest single day of the Civil War. In the woods and fields along Antietam Creek lay the crumpled corpses of 2,108 Union soldiers and 1,546 Confederates. The total number of killed, wounded, and missing men was more than 22,000. Across the battlefield, injured men moaned and cried out for help. In crude field hospitals, army surgeons sawed off mangled arms and legs. With bandages and kind attention, nurse Clara Barton saved the lives of as many as she could.

Clara Barton

On the evening of September 18, the Confederate army silently withdrew from

The Battle of Antietam was the bloodiest single day of the Civil War.

Sharpsburg. General Lee's weary troops crossed the Potomac River and returned to Virginia. From his headquarters, General McClellan claimed Union victory. Though more Union than Confederate men had been lost in the battle, Lee's Confederate invasion of the North had been stopped. Instead of chasing after the retreating southerners, however, McClellan let his battered army rest. In Washington, D.C., President Lincoln told the members of his cabinet, "The rebels . . . have been driven out of Maryland . . ."

The frightful bloodshed at Sharpsburg soon gave the war a deeper meaning than ever before. After a long summer of Union defeats, Lincoln seized this moment of success to issue an important document. On September 22, he signed the Emancipation Proclamation. This presidential order proclaimed that beginning on January 1, 1863, "all persons held as slaves

After the battle, President Lincoln (in top hat) traveled to Antietam to meet with General McClellan (sixth from left).

The Emancipation Proclamation

within any State . . . in rebellion against the United States, shall be then, thenceforth, and forever free."

Before the Battle of Antietam, the North had been fighting only to save the Union. In the days ahead, however, the Union army could march proudly into battle knowing that the war would also abolish slavery. The North and South would struggle on dozens of other battlefields during the next two and a half years. But General Lee's Confederate surrender to Union General Ulysses S. Grant at Appomattox Courthouse, Virginia, on April 9, 1865, would at last fulfill the promise made in blood beside Antietam Creek.

INDEX

PHOTO CREDITS

Cover, Library of Congress: 1, AP/Wide World; 2, MOLLUS/U.S. Army Military History Institute; 3, 4, 5 (both photos), North Wind; 6, © Jim Reber/Antietam National Battlefield; 7, Historical Pictures/Stock Montage; 8 (top), North Wind; 8 (bottom), Bureau of Engraving and Printing; 9 (top), Picture Bank; 9 (bottom), Historical Pictures/Stock Montage; 11, MOLLUS/USAMHI: 12 (top), North Wind; 12 (bottom), MOLLUS-USAMHI; 13 (both photos), North Wind; 14 (top), The Bettmann Archive; 14 (bottom), Historical Pictures/Stock Montage; 15 (top), North Wind; 15 (bottom), The Bettmann Archive; 16 (top), MOLLUS-USAMHI; 16 (bottom), The Bettmann Archive; 17 (top), MOLLUS-USAMHI; 17 (bottom), MOLLUS-USAMHI; 18-19, © Larry Sherer; 19 (bottom), 21 (left), North Wind; 21 (right), 22 (bottom), MOLLUS-USAMHI; 22 (top), Historical Pictures/Stock Montage; 23, The Bettmann Archive; 24 (both photos), 25, 26, 27, 28 (bottom), Historical Pictures/Stock Montage; 28 (top), MOLLUS-USAMHI; 29 (top), American Antiquarian Society; 29 (bottom), MOLLUS-USAMHI; 30, Historical Pictures/Stock Montage; 31, Library of Congress

Picture Identifications:
Cover: Union troops at Antietam after the battle
Page 1: The bodies of Confederate artillerymen near the Dunker church
Page 2: Union signal corpsmen man an observation post near Sharpsburg on the day before the battle.

Project Editor: Shari Joffe
Designer: Karen Yops
Cornerstones of Freedom Logo: David Cunningham

ABOUT THE AUTHOR

Zachary Kent grew up in Little Falls, New Jersey, and received a degree in English from St. Lawrence University. After college, he worked at a New York City literary agency for two years and then launched his writing career. Mr. Kent has written many books for Childrens Press.